accent on

SOLOS

COMPLETE

by
william gillock

ISBN 978-1-4950-7921-4

EXCLUSIVELY DISTRIBUTED BY

HAL•LEONARD®

Visit Hal Leonard Online at
www.halleonard.com

Contact us:
Hal Leonard
7777 West Bluemound Road
Milwaukee, WI 53213
Email: info@halleonard.com

In Europe, contact:
Hal Leonard Europe Limited
42 Wigmore Street
Marylebone, London, W1U 2RN
Email: info@halleonardeurope.com

In Australia, contact:
Hal Leonard Australia Pty. Ltd.
4 Lentara Court
Cheltenham, Victoria, 3192 Australia
Email: info@halleonard.com.au

CONTENTS

Up and Down the Keyboard

Words and Music by
William Gillock

LEVEL 1

Steadily

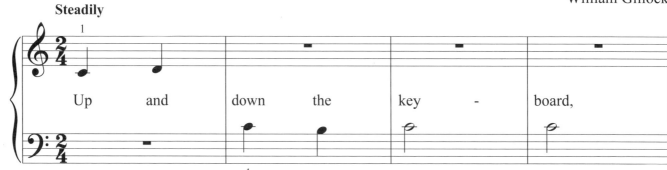

Up   and   down   the   key - board,

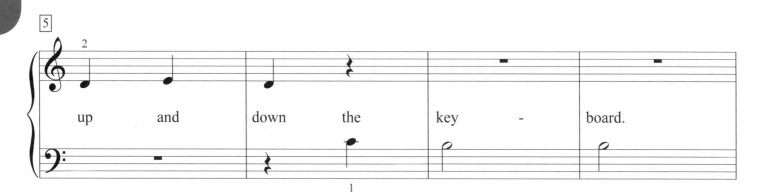

up   and   down   the   key - board.

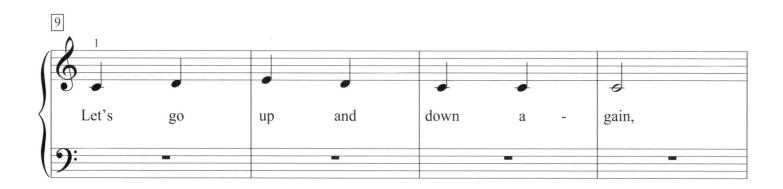

Let's   go   up   and   down   a - gain,

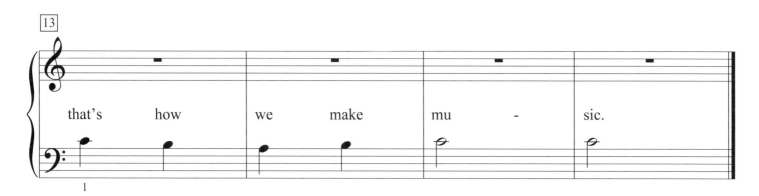

that's   how   we   make   mu - sic.

Puppy Dog

Words and Music by
William Gillock

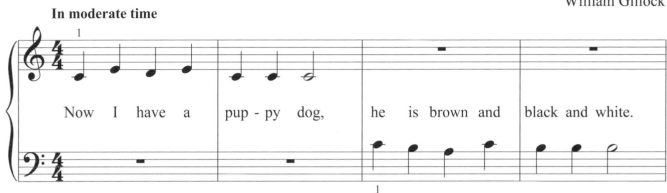

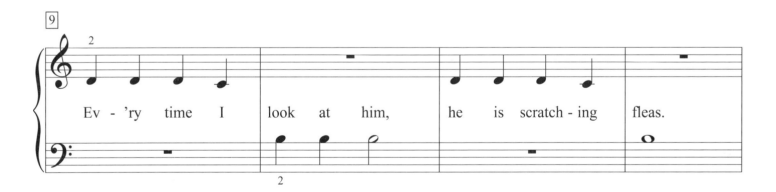

Circus Clown

Words by Steina Stratton
Music by William Gillock

In moderate time

Best of all I like the clown, jump - ing, tum - bling, fall - ing down.

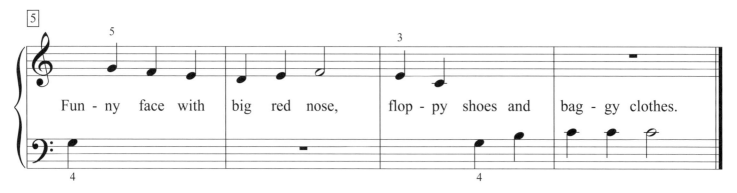

Fun - ny face with big red nose, flop - py shoes and bag - gy clothes.

Snowman

Words by Steina Stratton
Music by William Gillock

In walking time

Snow- man, snow- man, you're such fun! Glad you came to - day.

You're a friend to ev - 'ry - one. Please, oh please, don't melt a - way.

Halloween Witch

Words by Steina Stratton
Music by William Gillock

Little Brass Band

Words and Music by
William Gillock

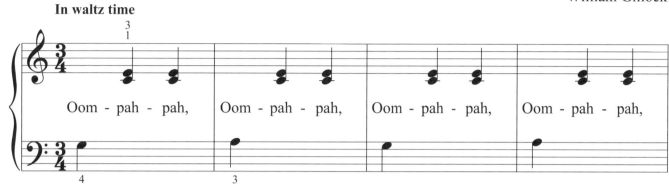

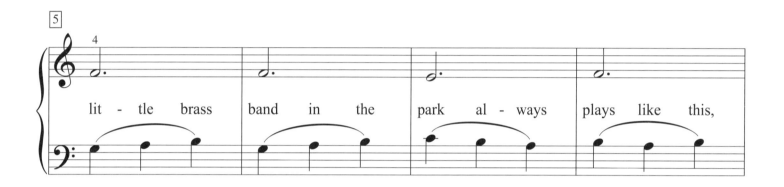

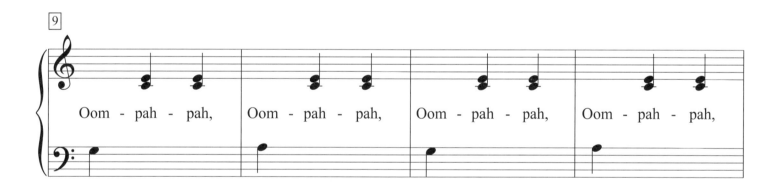

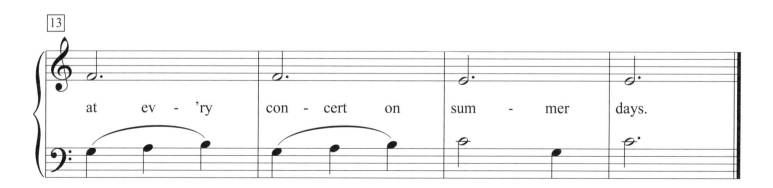

Daddy's Rocking Chair

Words by Dorothy Brin Crocker
Music by William Gillock

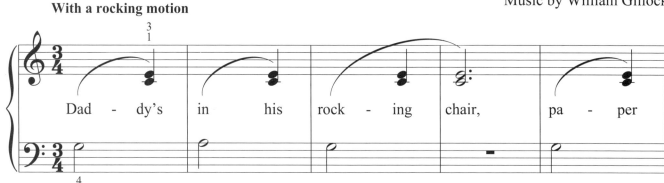

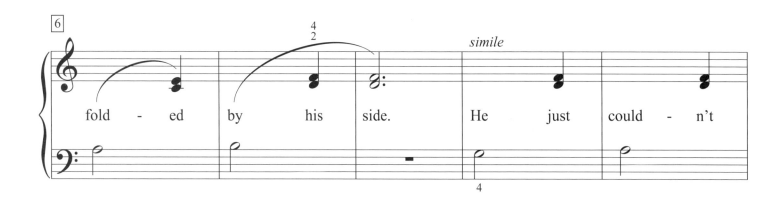

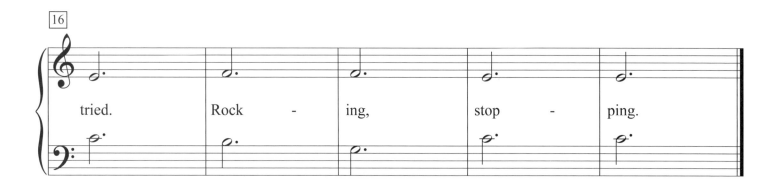

Glass Beads

Words and Music by
William Gillock

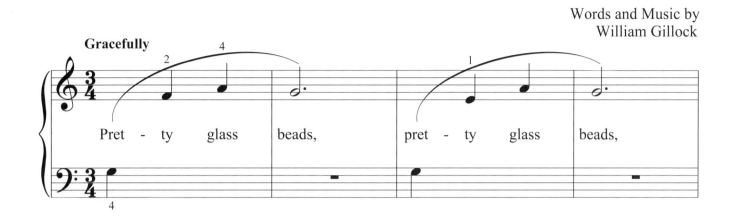

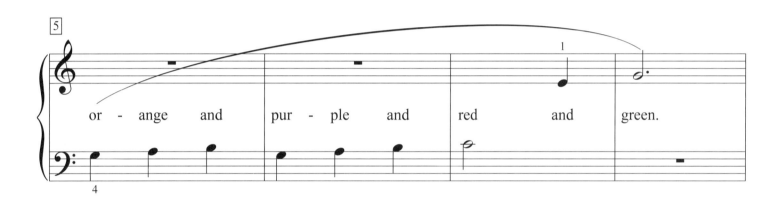

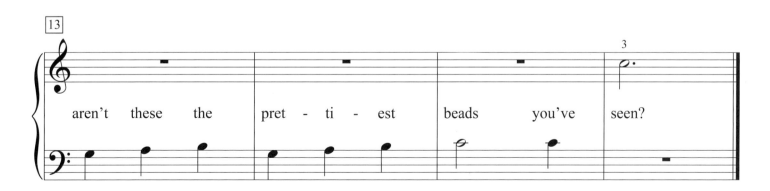

State Fair

Words and Music by
William Gillock

In march time

Trum - pet - ers, drum - mers too, all are pass - ing in re - view.

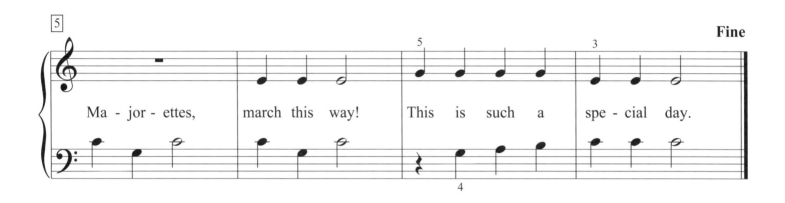

Ma - jor - ettes, march this way! This is such a spe - cial day.

Fine

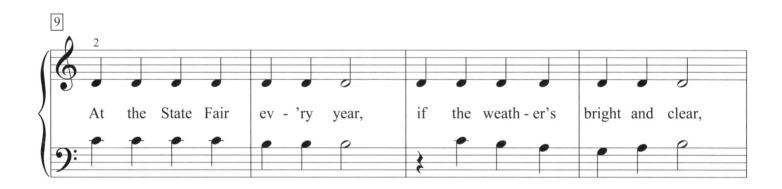

At the State Fair ev - 'ry year, if the weath - er's bright and clear,

we take all the fun - ny rides and laugh un - til we split our sides!

D.C. al Fine

Flying Carpet

Words by Dorothy Brin Crocker
Music by William Gillock

In a lilting manner

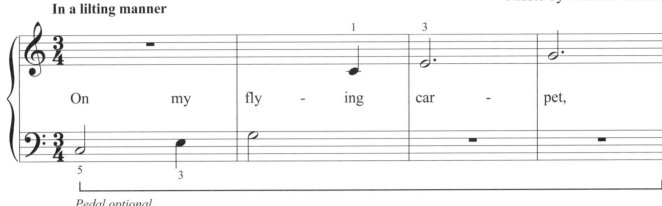

Pedal optional

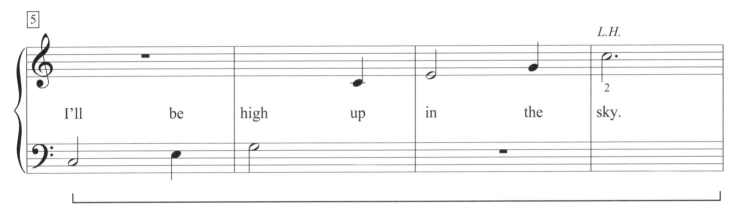

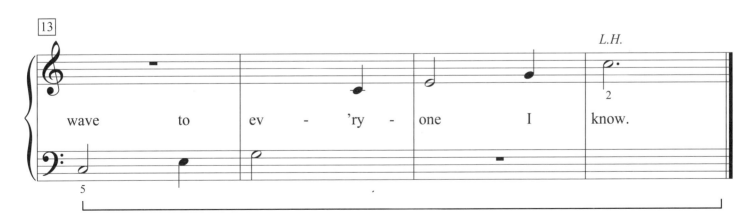

Clocks and Watches

Words and Music by
William Gillock

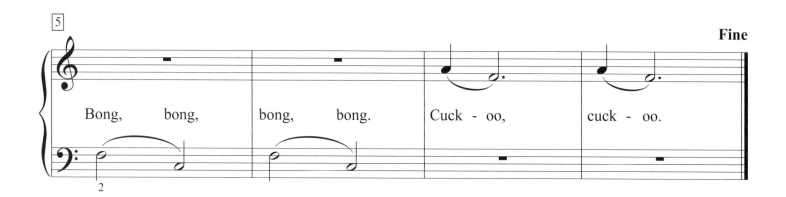

Winter Wind

Words by Steina Stratton
Music by William Gillock

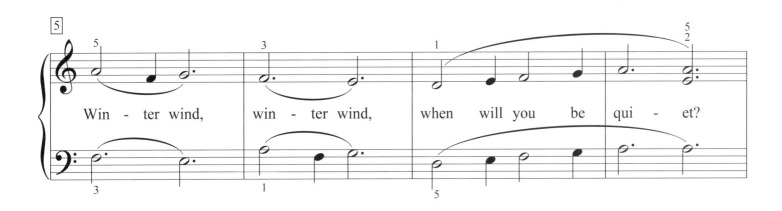

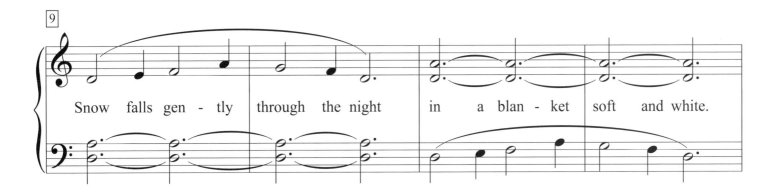

Wind in the Bamboo Tree

Words and Music by
William Gillock

Softly, with gentle movement

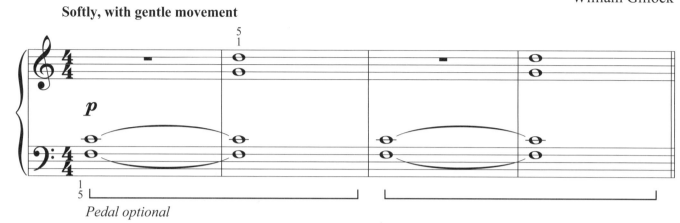

Pedal optional

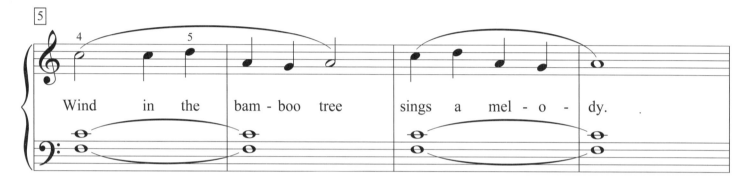

Wind in the bam - boo tree sings a mel - o - dy.

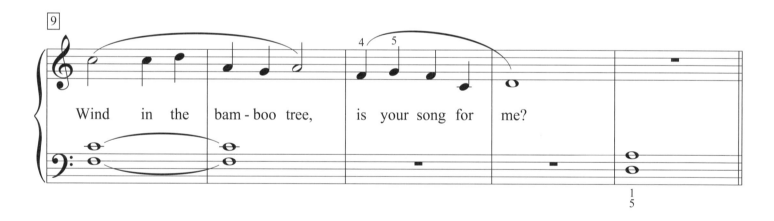

Wind in the bam - boo tree, is your song for me?

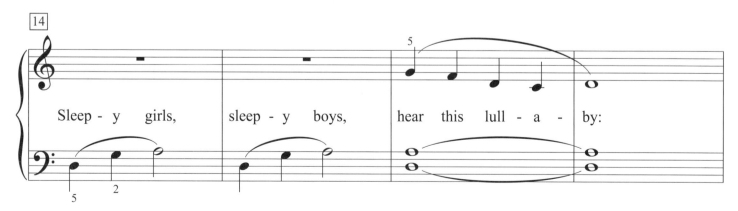

Sleep - y girls, sleep - y boys, hear this lull - a - by:

"Gen - tly sleep, gen - tly sleep," soft - ly it sighs.

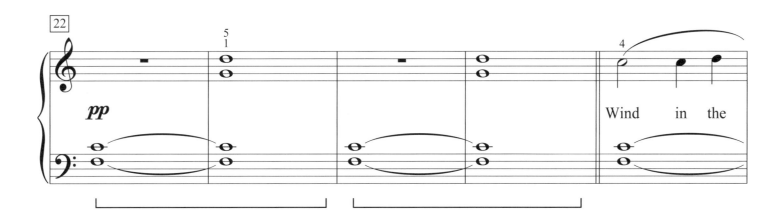

pp

Wind in the

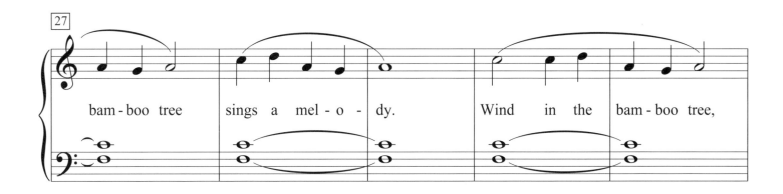

bam - boo tree sings a mel - o - dy. Wind in the bam - boo tree,

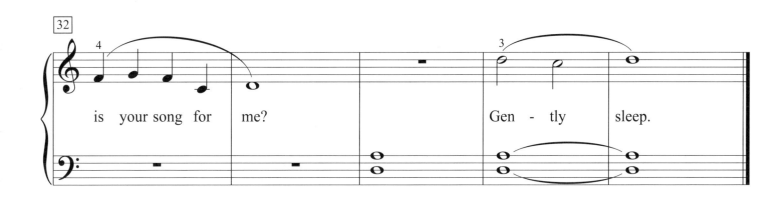

is your song for me? Gen - tly sleep.

Rain Dance

William Gillock

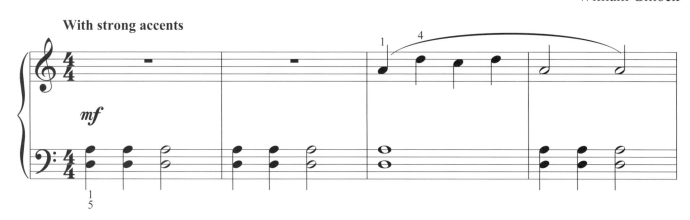

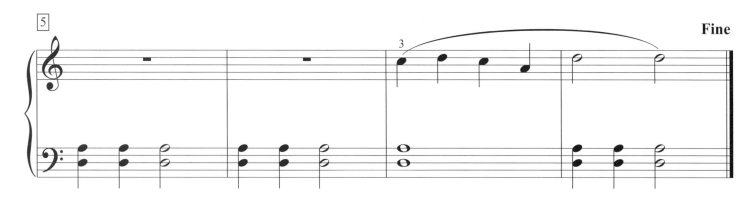

Summertime Polka

William Gillock

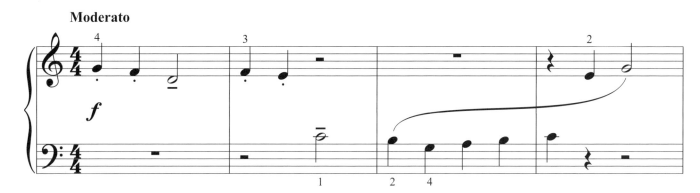

Little Gray Donkey

William Gillock

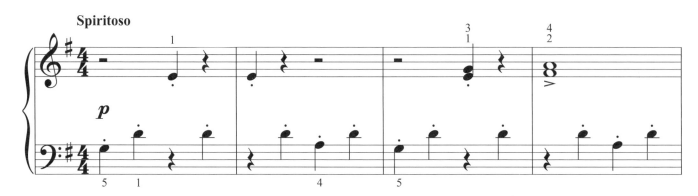

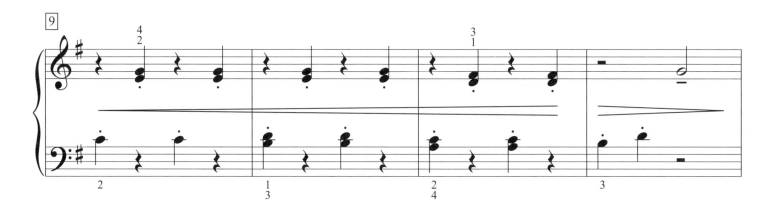

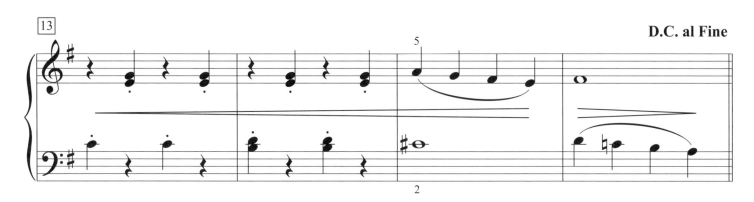

Peace Chant

William Gillock

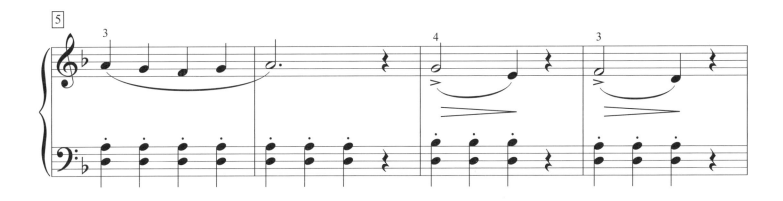

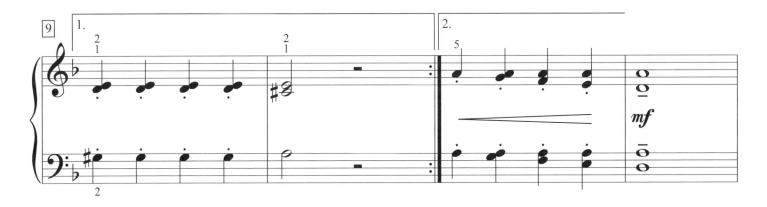

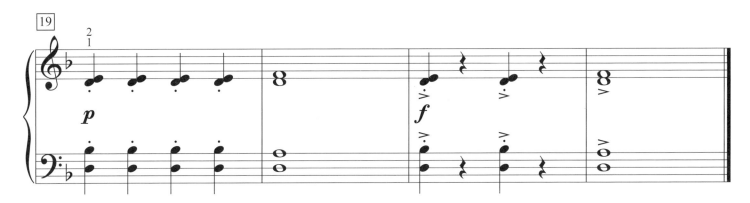

Little Flower Girl of Paris

William Gillock

Tempo di valse

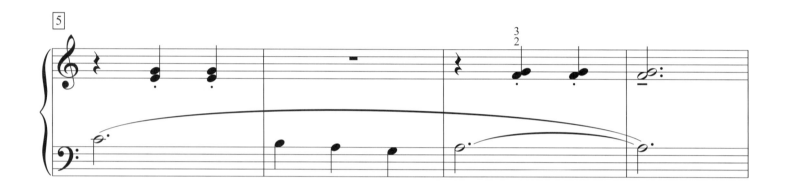

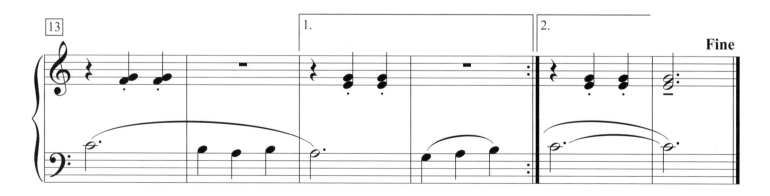

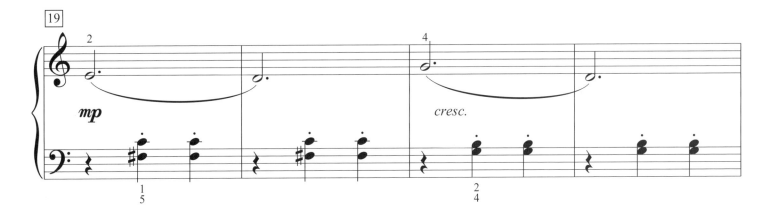

D.C. al Fine

Splashing in the Brook

William Gillock

Sail Boats

William Gillock

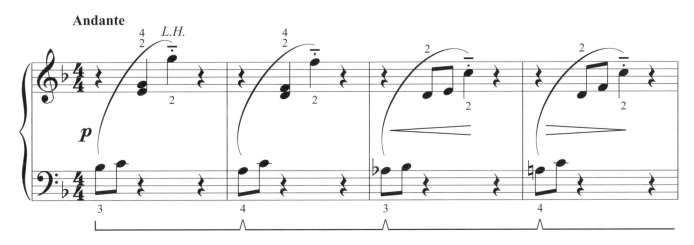

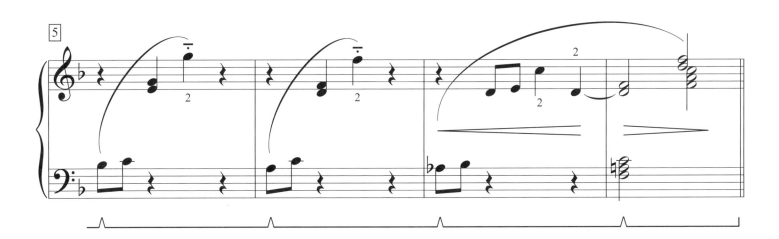

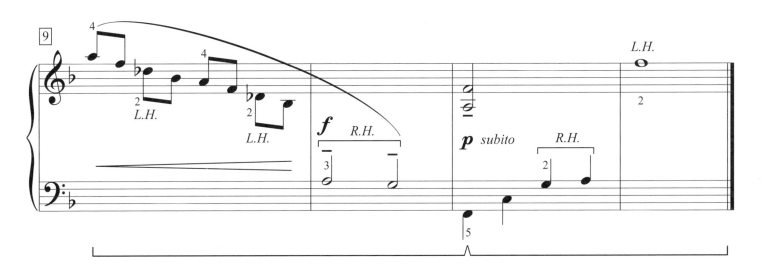

Dance Under the Stars

William Gillock

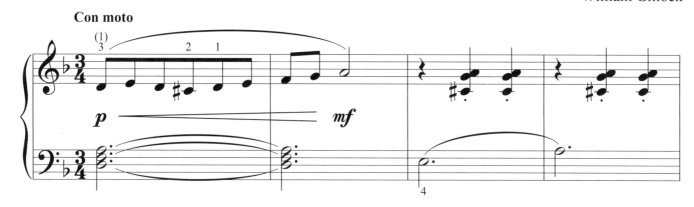

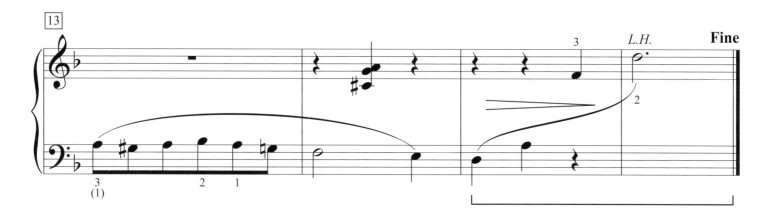

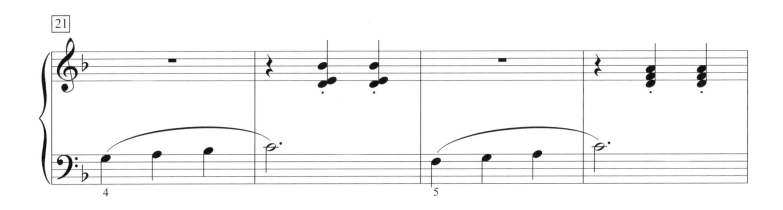

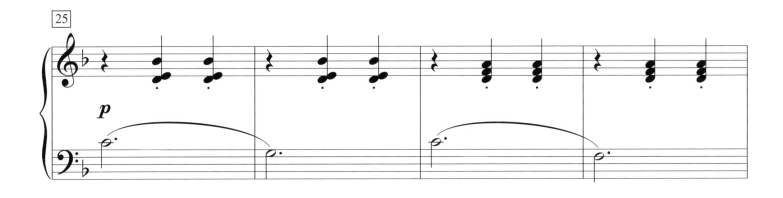

D.C. al Fine

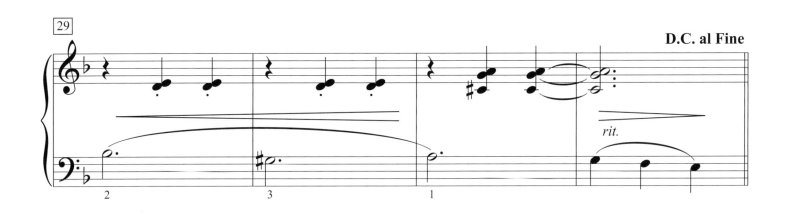

Argentina

William Gillock

Stars on a Summer Night

William Gillock

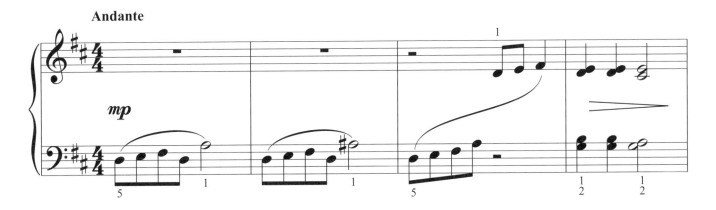

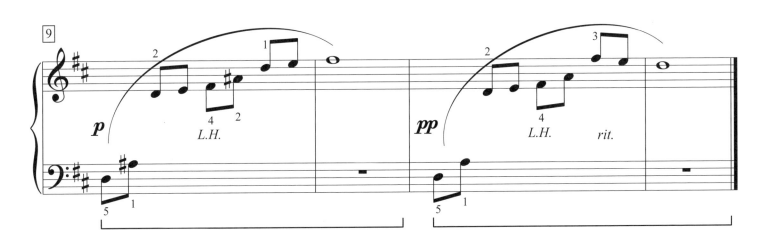

Gavotte and Musette

William Gillock

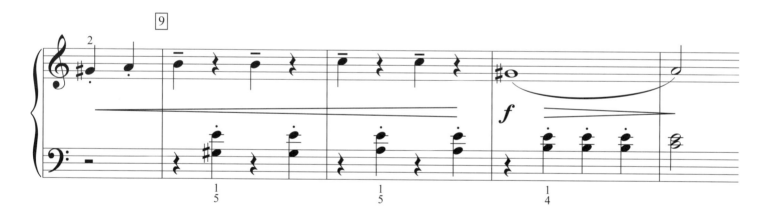

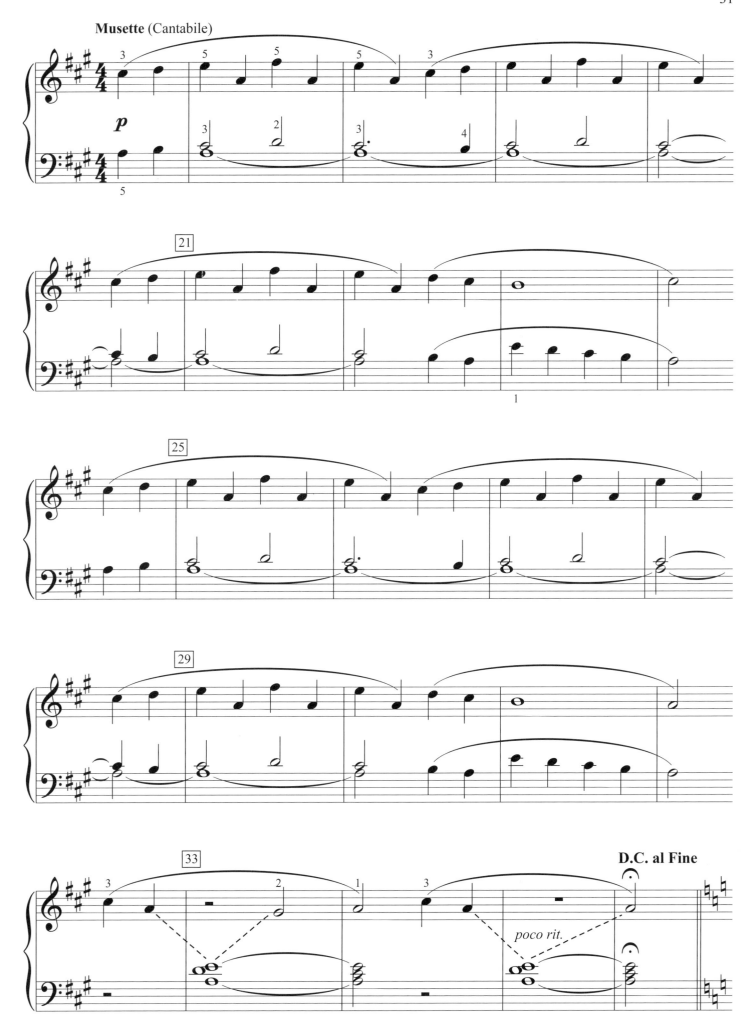

Owl at Midnight

William Gillock

Andante misterioso

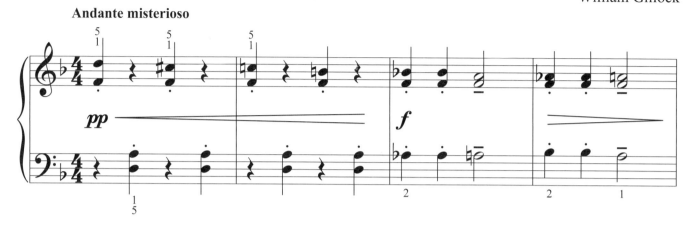

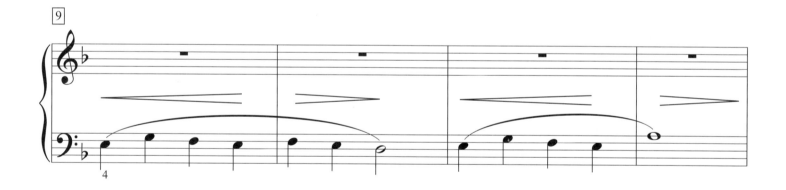

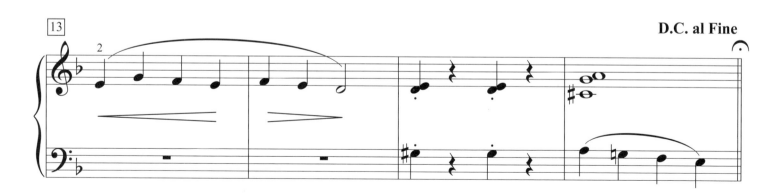

Drifting Clouds

William Gillock

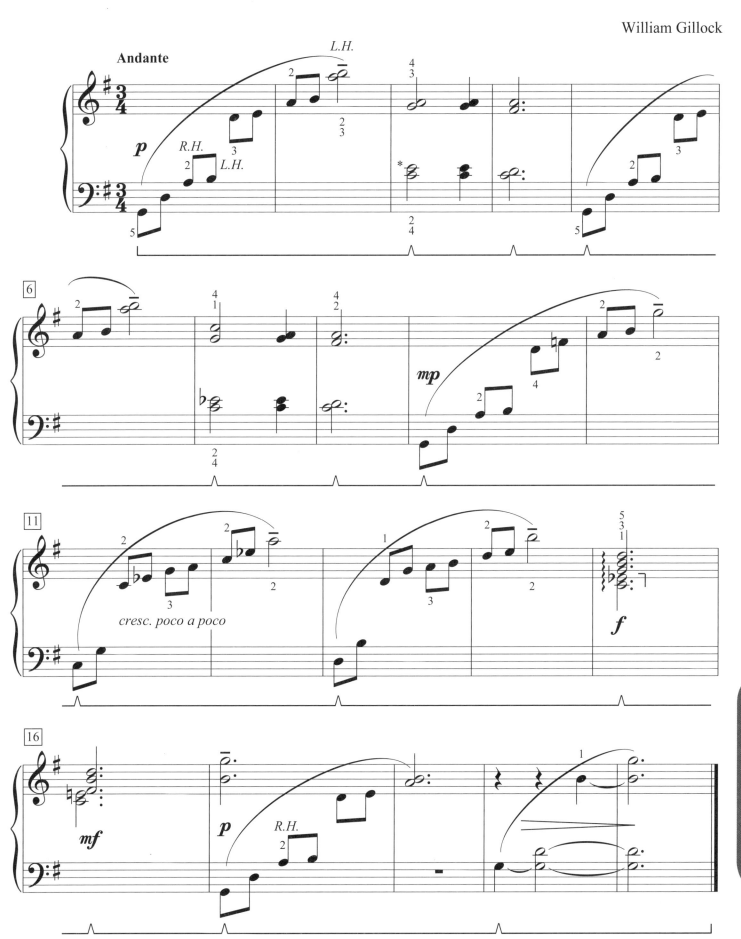

*Originally written as E-flat; Gillock revised in 1993.

LEVEL 3

Sliding in the Snow

William Gillock

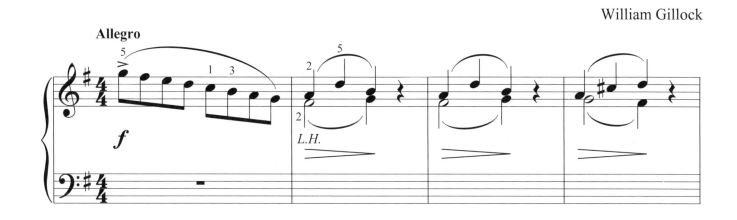

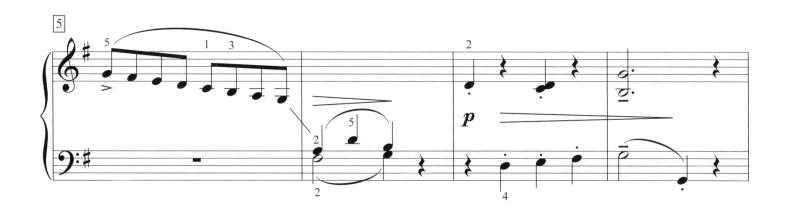

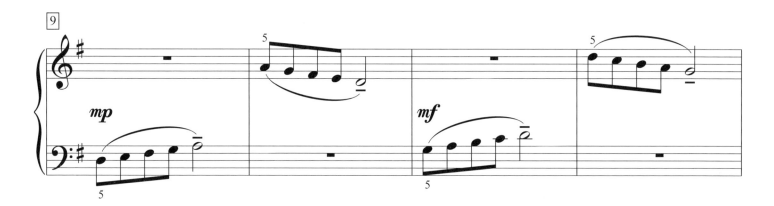

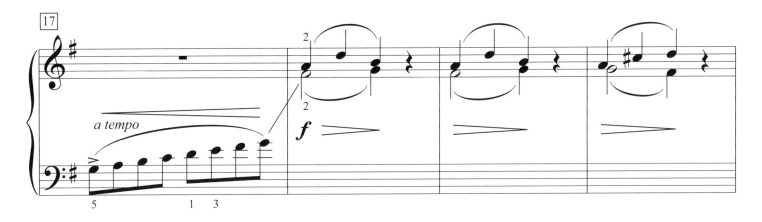

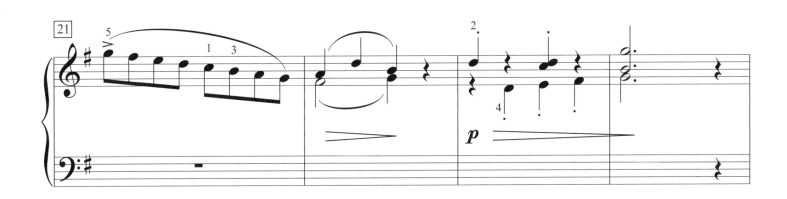

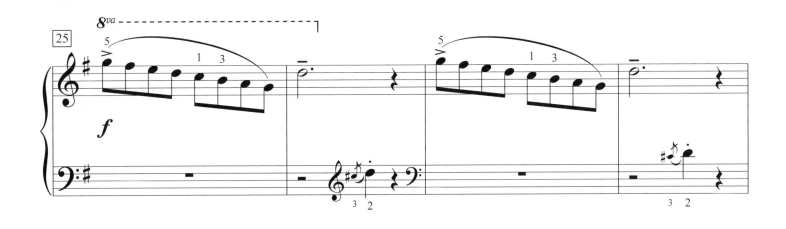

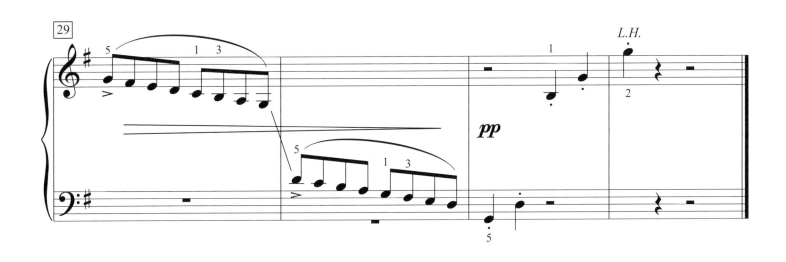

The Queen's Minuet

William Gillock

Tempo di menuetto

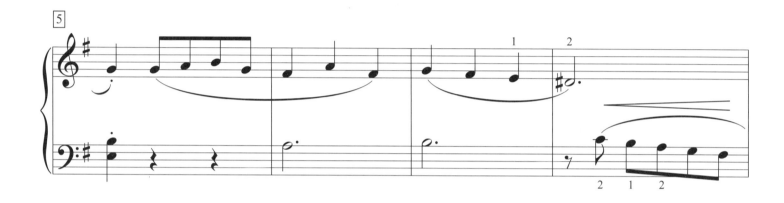

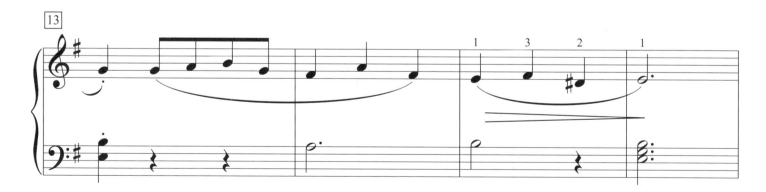

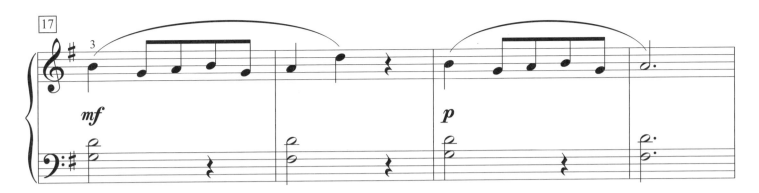

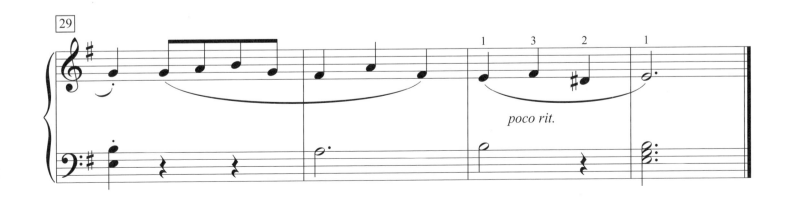

At the Circus

William Gillock

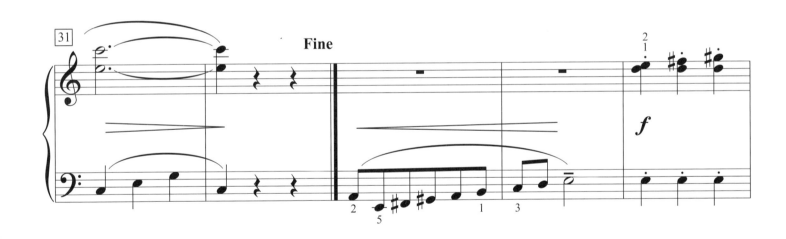

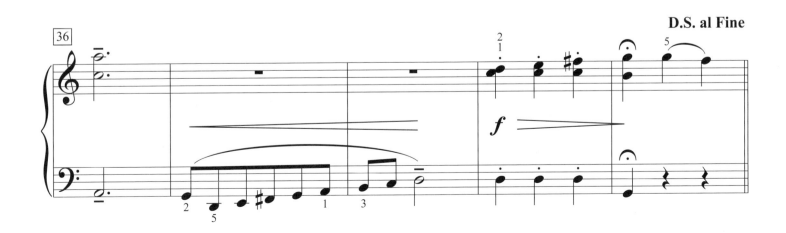

Swinging Beat

William Gillock

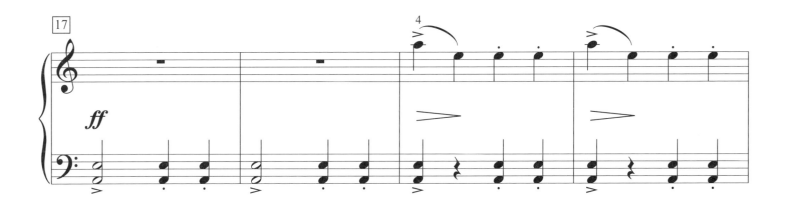

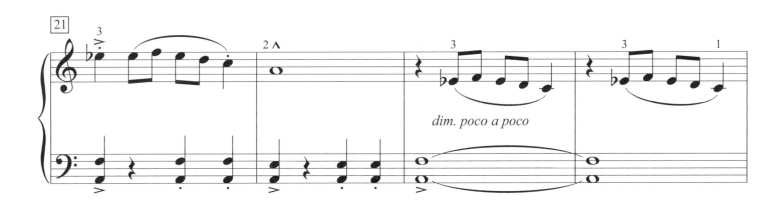

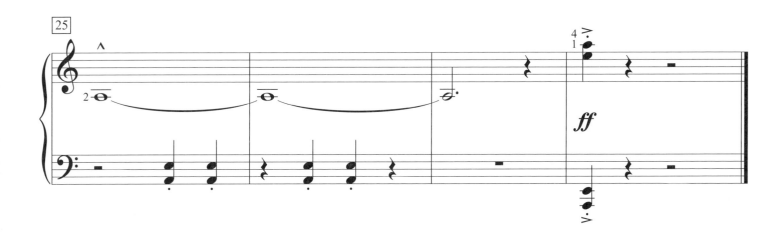

Dance of the Toys

William Gillock

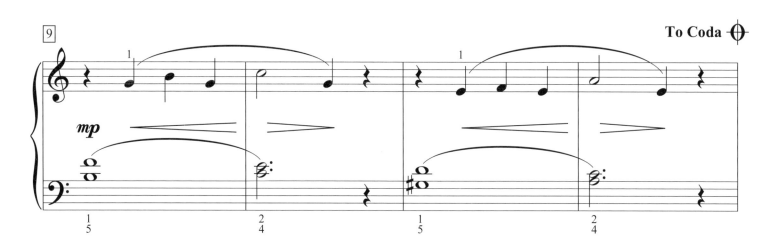

D.C. al Coda

CODA

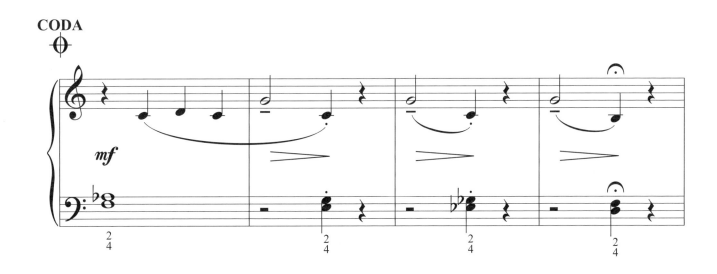

Enchanting Marketplace

William Gillock

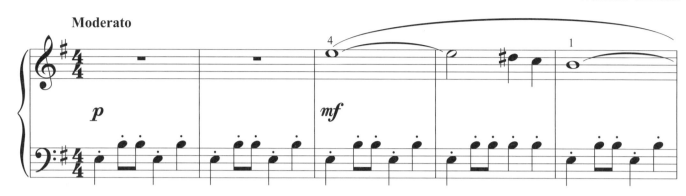

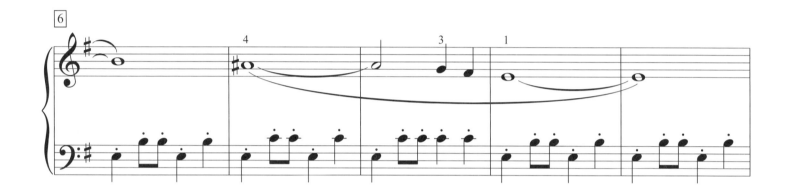

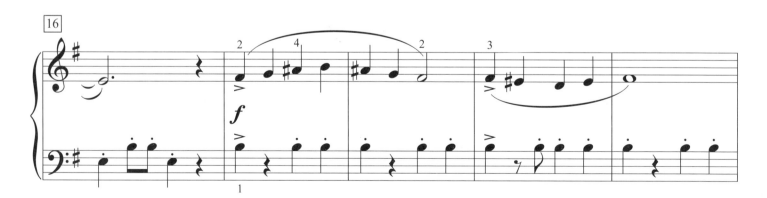

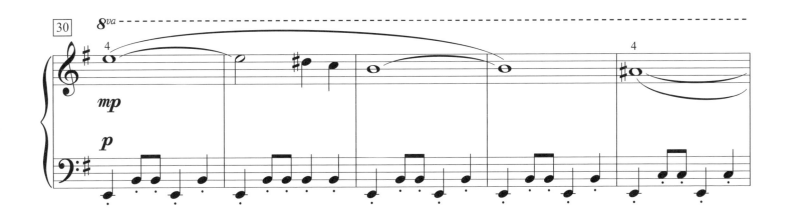

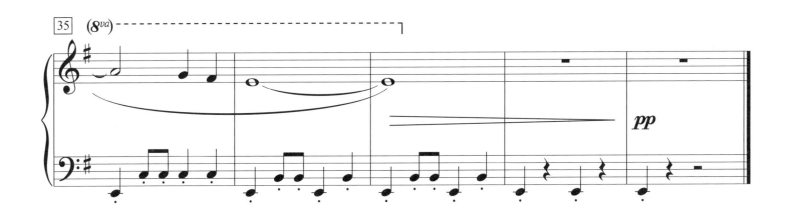

Summertime Blues

William Gillock